M000191623

REF~~~~~~

REFUSENIK

LYNN MELNICK

YESYES BOOKS, PORTLAND

REFUSENIK © 2022 BY LYNN MELNICK

COVER & INTERIOR DESIGN: ALBAN FISCHER

ISBN 978-1-936919-88-8

PRINTED IN THE UNITED STATES OF AMERICA

PUBLISHED BY YESYES BOOKS

1614 NE ALBERTA ST

PORTLAND, OR 97211

YESYESBOOKS.COM

KMA SULLIVAN, PUBLISHER

STEVIE EDWARDS, SENIOR EDITOR, BOOK DEVELOPMENT

ALBAN FISCHER, GRAPHIC DESIGNER

COLE HILDEBRAND, MANAGING EDITOR

ALEXIS SMITHERS, ASSISTANT EDITOR

AMBER RAMBHAROSE, ASSISTANT EDITOR, INSTAGRAM

JAMES SULLIVAN, ASSISTANT EDITOR, AUDIO BOOKS

PHILLIP B. WILLIAMS, COEDITOR IN CHIEF, *VINYL*

AMIE ZIMMERMAN, EVENTS COORDINATOR

for Anita & Michael Melnick

for Evelyn & Lester Melnick
for Shirley & Saul Goldberger

& all the Melnicks, Weissmans, Lazarowitzes, Piclarius, Rosenbergs, Hirschbergs, Goldbergers, Seligmanns, Mandls, Werners, Kaufmanns, Gorlickis, Nasches, and Wormsers

who taught me to refuse

To my readers: this is a book about trauma and survival.
Please be aware that it contains scenes of rape and other violence.

CONTENTS

re·fuse·nik
rəˈfyo͞oznik/
noun

1.

a person and especially a Jew in the former Soviet Union who was refused permission to emigrate

2.

a person who refuses to follow orders or obey the law, especially as a protest

THE NIGHT OF THE MURDERED POETS

I am writing this on a plane
to California

with several pens in my bag
and all the water I want.

It was evening when I left
and will be evening when I get there.

Sometimes I look at photos of myself
and wonder why I was not smiling.

It's hard to imagine we once mattered so much
that they'd round us up. I mean poets.

I know Jews have often been rounded up.
I am contemplating

a vermin metaphor here
just because of how hard it is to get us

but I know better. I had to look up
"cosmopolitanism" in my dictionary.

Forgive me, I did have a school but I didn't
show up much. I was too busy

trying to murder myself.
Stalin thought cosmopolitanism contemptible

and Jewish.
Want to demolish the core of a community?

Once upon a time,
you could simply kill the poets.

But more poets arose in their place.
Well, more poets arose in this place

I should say. I was growing—what
is the word for something that grows

peculiar and withstanding?—
in California like the orange tree

not native to the soil.
The first poem I wrote

was about bleeding from my uterus
onto glare-drenched stairs.

After the poets died
in a prison basement

the Soviets smashed the Yiddish
linotype machines.

I had to look up "linotype."
When I left pencils behind

I bought myself a typewriter.
I'm writing this on a laptop in the sky.

After the poets died
the location of their remains was kept secret

from their families;
their families were exiled to Siberia,

their families were social outcasts.
I only just learned about this.

I was a social outcast as a girl.
I'd get so high I'd forget to brush my teeth.

I want to remember how ill-starred
the prison basement

as I imagine it. I am finishing this on a plane
from California. It was afternoon

when I left and will be night
when I get home.

I believe in little
but I always say the Sh'ma on airplanes.

I want to remember
that we'll never know the murder weapon

but we do know it, of course,
dozens of metaphors deep. I want to remember

that until recently
I didn't know any of this.

THE ONLY JEW AT THE MOCK JEWISH WEDDING

My friend's missing father came from Mexico
but her mom wouldn't confirm it.

Sometimes she insisted Greece
sometimes Peru. Eventually

we found proof in a Ziploc of documents.
We also found a stash of pills and money.

We took our giddy selves to the McDonald's
on Wilshire near Fairfax

and I ordered the first treyf I ever ate.
It felt less momentous than I wanted it to.

At the mock Jewish weddings they serve pig.
It's hard to tell if it's meant to taunt

or just that in Radzanow
there are animals one expects to consume.

My maternal ancestors
told people they were from glam Vienna

but they were not.
They were from peasant Poland.

The dictionary qualifies *shtetl* as
"(*formerly*)"

but we never left. I once broke into a ballroom
at the Plaza

and all I could think to do
was put my boots up on a fainting couch.

Even at mock Jewish weddings most fetish bores me
but I suppose it's a comfort

to burlesque the joy of what you murdered.

Who are we trying to trick here?
I mean this to be answered.

How are we different? This too.
There is so much bacon in the world.

We came to this country
to pioneer having it all

then we forgot why we started
our own country clubs,

white hands tapping cigar ash
at another lavish reception.

Assimilation is quick. Also impossible.
In Ukraine, where Melnicks originate,

figurines of Jews
are sold as good luck charms.

In America, I'm hanging on inside my own pocket.
I dare you to watch me parade my costume

here. I am not particle underneath.

If there is no Torah in the synagogue
I am still proof it is a building.

GETTING ON

I don't need to be told
my body is not what my body
was, descending, live wire,

the option to light.
People keep telling me
it's my ass

or my face but it's neither
and it's both.
Tell me what to do

about sliding into oblivion
about what is material
and what will be remembered.

Aging is a motherfucker,
I say to myself.
I fuck myself, I mother.

When I'm alone
I document that I was here
while I'm still here.

WHEN BAD THINGS HAPPEN TO GOOD PEOPLE

You can only hear *you look like a hooker* so many times
before you become one. Spandex was really big

the year I stopped believing.
I babysat for the rabbi's son, Isaac. There was luxe carpet

in every room of the condo. Isaac liked Legos
and we made a pasture and a patriarch and lots of wives.

In his car in his garage the rabbi handed me a self-help book
and put my hand on his crotch, ready to go.

I didn't care.
I made good money.

Isaac lived to be 180 according to the bible.
Isaac is the only patriarch who didn't have concubines.

Isaac is 30 now. Modern scholarship tells us

the patriarchs never existed. Survival has taught me
the patriarchs are what we've got.

We were left alone when the massacre that carries some variation on my name
(but was titled for the Cossack who accused the Jews of having all the money)
ended. A faraway false messiah showed up to assure us we'd all be ok with

the nothing we had and the everything that was taken from us. No one was
watching out for debauchery in the town that lay in the midst of the hills at the
end of the world. A messiah should take a whore for a wife it was prophesied

so he said, so he did. Actual hell broke loose. In a later century, a man fled
Nazis and published his first story about messianic hedonism after the
Chmelnicki massacres. It was not an allegory. Those who seemed to be

possessed by evil, were. The author of the story became famous. An Orthodox
typesetter worried, "He's a pornographer!" He won the Nobel prize the year
my family moved to California. I stood diminutive on a line in a bookstore to

meet him while a man held the back of my neck to keep me still. The famous
author called me adorable, and I was, with crooked bangs and glaucous eyes.
Later I got sexy and so many men held the back of my neck that I began to

charge. It turned out there was no one coming to save any of us. We had to
answer for our own desperate pleasure. No one answered for the pain in the
back of my neck. I left Los Angeles because of the pain in the back of my neck

and moved to the city the famous author immortalized for its buildings and
brandies held by wanton and ruined women in thigh-high stockings at seances.
I bought blue wool fishnet stockings to prove my seductive winter practicality.

I told no one about my memories but instead wrote about them in my poems.
I published my very first poem with the line "there was a way to save me."
My second book was shelved as porn by a popular online bookstore. Once a

cab driver told me he would rape me if I'm Jewish and I said "I'm not" with
the same ease as the faraway false messiah (when forced by the Turks to
convert) lied to his captors. But life got good in New York, in my body, and I

forgot why my neck still hurts. My Catholic husband made me matzo ball soup
in winter. I let myself contemplate faith gone awry. He puzzles how I am still
surprised by the evil that men do. Our arguments stay the same year after year

because I can't talk about myself. He tucks me into bed each night where I
summon all the men, summon all the history, admit I will never be unworried,
will always wake fighting for my life.

INAUGURATION POEM

Do you know what it's like when a body twice yours
holds you down in the room where you make your life

until you wouldn't know how to move even if he wasn't
holding you down and then he splits you further open

and the world before

had been filled with its usual losses and rages not this

what is this do you know

what it's like when you live just one door away and every
time you have to step outside, well no, he's not there,

not now, but he could be and the dread is

everything for years

even when sometimes there is whisky and sometimes
there is joy, there is dread in the ficus tree on the landing

and dread in the weather-beaten flag by the garage
and dread in the cash inside the mattresses that are always

moving in and out

of the building next door and what if people call you
corny because you still hold onto details like all the gray

kitten posters on the gray walls of every quakeproof hospital
you were sent to to escape the dread and yet

even when they pumped you full of drugs and even when
they dried you out of them, there was always dread

and you were

and you will be

nose down in every room
in which you try to make your life?

FOREMOTHERS

I celebrated the new year
alone on a sofa eating Frosted Flakes while listening

to country music. I'm uncertain
what to call this form of worship.

No autumn has answered a question like this.
The world holds me up, finally, while beneath me

it crumbles under men and their monsters.
I won't genuflect towards anything I'm not also

prepared to pleasure.
Supplication makes me wince.

I don't care how many
Sarahs, Rebeccas, Rachels, and Leahs

any holy book wants to add to the modern retelling
or in how many sermons we reach hard

to find ways in which these wives counted.
I don't want to be tacked on in fair practice

and I'm done looking up synonyms for patriarchy
in part because there are none.

TINSELTOWN

All the beige apartment buildings
with absurd little windows
despite the glow they could let in:
I get those buildings.
I formed all my bad ideas in those buildings
then I took them to the streets.

Yesterday I stood and I snapped
the outdated GIRLS DANCE sign overhanging
a parking lot outside a pop-up restaurant
people feel so fancy about
they are willing to wait to eat
when they never want for food.

Girls did dance, I assure you. Late century
we all felt the pop-metal backbeat
supersede our hearts, but
simpler times!
I mean, as kids we could walk into bars,
throw some quarters into vending machines

and pull the knob out for Kents
or whatever mistakenly fell.
The bartenders didn't not give us matches.
We didn't not give them blow jobs.
This was before the sharing economy
or else what if maybe we invented it.

WE'D LIKE TO KNOW A LITTLE BIT
ABOUT YOU FOR OUR FILES

I am terrible at upkeep.
I don't shave any part of me.

I exist!
I just read an article about Jewish men who prefer to nail shiksas

to stiffen their assimilation.
Is there anyone living

who has heard of a shegetz?
I want to be beautiful.

I am Semitic beautiful.
There's no denying this face or how many would enter it.

Recently I watched two blond women
brush each other's hair on a couch at a waterfront bar.

I think sometimes
of the red-headed actor who sat across from me

in a Pico Boulevard coffeehouse
claiming Jewish women have the kind of swollen cunts

that beg to be fucked.
I just read an article about Jewish men in Hollywood

who assault women they work with.
I'm always curious

when what men have to say is
no comment.

GLASNOST BOWL

One summer I walked to a field to watch boys
    run practice drills. I was 13. We girls drank beer

in the bleachers and followed those small bodies
    in big shoulder pads scatter back and forth

across a stretch of land like the larval graphics our eyes
    clung to in the earliest 80s arcade games.

First rule of America is you can't imagine everywhere
    doesn't want to be here. Papers boasted Soviets

were curious how many people die during our game
    which is a trick question. My grandmother taught me

football is for the goyim, which meant probably
    it's American, and I didn't tell her about the boys,

their drills and the beer. Meanwhile, Soviet infrastructure
    didn't allow for exhibition because infrastructure

didn't exist there. The game moved to LA.
    Holy all that is capitalism, we craved publicity.

The world seemed to start and end in California.
    At least on TV. The star of the Bowl later put a bullet

in his own chest. Brain trauma. He beat his wife.
    I was 20 when another football player killed his wife

and I watched it unfold on TV north of the city where
    I failed to flee a man of my own. He was also an athlete.

I've never tried to bury anything so much
    in my life as my own unsafety and the spectacle

of a famous wife's death. Los Angeles was good to me.
    Scandal was for the goyim. Publicity is for America.

My own bruised torso didn't exist. First rule of America is
    strong men pretend to look out for you.

Los Angeles lost, but won the rematch. The sun licked
    our skin on days so mild I still dissociate with familiarity

then tire trying to get myself back. What would I tell
    the girl in the bleachers, buzzed on America? I've already

closed the tab on the Soviets, on the '80s, on beer.
    First rule of Los Angeles is you need an audience.

First rule of America is you have to face it head on
    like a man while men charge at you, while men send you

to the hospital between apologies and excuses and the
    ER nurse who impatiently whispers *Next time he'll kill you.*

LOSING THE NARRATIVE

A shattered bottle tore through my hand last month and slit
a vein until every finger was purple and I couldn't

make even a tentative fist. I used the other hand to indicate

I'm okay.

How unwise I am, how polite in a crisis.
In triage, an overheard photo of someone's lover

almost 3000 miles west made me seize with longing
when I spied a palm tree in the background.

I understand what it says about me
that my body lustfully wishes to place itself

where it was never safe.

I have put enormous energy into trying to convince you
I'm fine and

I'm just about there, no?

Besides, decades on, poorly healed bones help me to predict rain
though it's true I like to verify weather

with another source because I know not to trust myself.
I've been told repeatedly I don't have a mind for plot but

it would be a clever twist, wouldn't it, if in the end I realize
it's me who does me in.

NEW YORK CITY, 1994

I fell in love with a city in summer
the smell of piss
and sweat down into the tunnels
intoxicating and I rode
cinema to cinema to eat candy in the dark.
I met a woman who kissed me suddenly

outside the discount theater
but I pulled away after a while
to pin my hair up
off my neck
and check my watch
(a city in summer undoes time)

before she invited me to hear demos
of songs about her dog
and, I know, right this moment
you are just about as bored as I was
but hear me out:
she had air conditioning

and let me lie naked across her bed
(I didn't need sleep those months) so
I weltered a bit aroused
over and under
sheets and it was okay! I *liked* the sounds
of the street, the trucks

grunting up Broadway, the impassioned
chatter of drunk people
not ready to give in, the deceptive
cooing from the roof and
all of it, though
I still can't tell you exactly why.

CANNIBAL ISLAND

What must be a mythology: Siberia.
In my imagination
take away the fur coats

and the finally locked lips
under the extremity of strings
and you've got a bunch of union men

removing set pieces and a sweaty actor
against a palm trying
to force a pack of matches to work.

At Paramount, I humped a man
who'd rip the filters off his Marlboros
and ohh how I thought it was cool.

It was backlot. He was beautiful.
His hands were always moving.
My world view started bleak then jubilant

letting myself cum against his hip bone.
If he only knew a fraction of what there was
to know about me then.

There is a folktale: fortress.
The Soviets named the horror
the Nazino affair, which suggests

a spy caper or a dime store novel
but it was thousands of political prisoners
and small-time crooks on a northbound

train to be resettled on a swampy island
with no access to necessities, which could only
end in disaster. I know

because I'm watching a film about it
while my husband is out of town.
I lapped up the quiet

for just minutes and now
I miss his body near mine.
The prettiest woman on the island

was protected by a prison guard
until he went to search for food.
Then she was strung up, her breasts

cut off, her muscles cut out, everything,
everything they could use.
There is a fact: *everywhere,*

there is always an angle, loneliness
isn't always a disaster but people,
people are always hungry.

AMERICAN VALUE INN

This route has tolls, predicts a sign
on I-80. I tell him dirty stories
and almost run us off the road.

We pull into a rest stop to take care of him.
It is never enough.
We pull into a diner parking lot and he wants more.

I have to be invisible, inconspicuous
soft suction out of nowhere.
Years later he'll track me down

to New York City using sorcery and wit
and he'll storm into the office
where I'll answer phones all day

with my flawed inflection. I digress.
When we get to a motel
he goes to piss while I strip

and lay on my back across the bed
even though history tells me what the spread
will feel like against my shell.

I stare at the wood paneling glued unevenly,
at the peek of off-white wall underneath
which forms shapes I turn

into visions, like clouds, like prophecy.
He appears around the corner,
rote for a moment. He is often cruel.

He is often tender. He flies at me
because he is a bat after dark
with his fangs and we are so far from lights

that I forget how precarious my durability.
He lifts me on top of him
and I am at it again. I cum. I digress,

I can, if I can, leave this room behind.

Yes, I believe in generational trauma plus that mix of pride and fear that 40+
years in patriarchy didn't fix. I have a hard time saying no because you all
are going to take it anyway but I didn't come to monologue that. Synopsis: I

am worried all the time because of the tsar. Synopsis: I want to talk about my
childhood devotion to *Fiddler on the Roof*. Sounds crazy, no? But I didn't
come here to choreograph how once I was so lost I couldn't leave the

apartment and there was food trash on the floor and mice were feasting on the
buffet and I wanted to die but didn't have the energy. Think about how our
whole cast of characters would have thrived with some Zoloft to swallow. I

pray to those pills most days; I'm gravely devout. I've got a shawl around
my head made of chemistry and pluck. Act 1: The Constable has sympathy
for the Jews, sure, but is powerless to prevent the violence. Who wants front

row seats? Do you adore that part where Tevye gets hammered and trades his
daughter for a cow? The Russian dancing is great. L'chaim! I know every
word of every song. I listened to that boxed set of albums so many times the

needle skipped at the wedding ballad but it didn't matter because eventually
I snapped both records in two. Sunrise, sunset. Passion, is what I'm saying.
Obsession. Ok, well, like with everything, I was in it for the sex. Musical

number: superstition turns me way on but mostly I wanted to run away with
the Marxist supporting character because, like for all of us cozy American
Jews, changing the world makes me wet. But I have to tell you, I don't think

I've ever had a Jewish cock in my pussy unless you count the one whose
wrong parent was Jewish. This is extraordinary math. All those women
deciding their own fate despite the master of the house making side deals

with Cossacks and yentas? The lights dim. Quiet, please, in the back, we've
arrived at Act 2: Tevye reaches deep into his soul, but he will not consent
to his daughter marrying a gentile. Fuck off with your agency, daughters!

What's a put-upon milkman supposed to do but bring that fiddler to America
to keep the girls in line and the tsar away. Cue the orchestra. Cue the aging
sound system. Holler "tradition" at me one more time, I dare you. Holler

"tradition" at me one more time and my rage will swallow all of America
and every last actor hamming up my damage to prove some folksy point
about conformity while the remains of us happen between blessing and

bruising as we swallow pills to make the inveterate fear dissolve, deliver
salvation to the craggy split of the vinyl reminder. Revival: I am not trying to
make a larger point as I have been too busy trying to keep panic down and

men out of range of this umpteenth curtain call to triumphantly bang out
what that might be.

WHY, BECAUSE THE DAZZLING SUN

It's one of those mornings
where everyone looks like someone
I have seen before—the man crossing the street

looks like the famous novelist who on TV said we're
not paying attention to the right things—the woman
heading down into the station looks like the woman

with whom I once spent a week who told me
she didn't like that we're the same height barefoot
because she'd prefer to be the smaller.

It appears I'm annoying
everyone today like it was my fault
the diner ran out of tens and I said *fives are okay*

sometimes fives are preferable and I smiled
but no one this morning thinks fives are okay.
I woke up knowing I would cry at everything.

I can see the train tracks from my bedroom window
and it's most of what keeps me plowing through winter.
I like comings and goings,

I like running away and returning darkly.
It would help enormously if people would stop
telling me I'm paying attention to the wrong things—

once a man said *good god, woman,*
you're obsessed! about my own orgasm
which he found me going after on his bathroom floor

but I just wanted one more. Is that obsession?
I have no answers this morning. I pause outside the diner
for the warmth on my skin

and a woman who looks like the woman
from whom I once almost bought a bedroom set says
He told me I'm too bitter!

into her phone and walks pointedly around me.
Is the hunt for pleasure always obsession?
I'm stalled here. I'm wallowing in sun.

For a while I wore baggy earth tone clothes because the last man I loved would strike me in the face if anyone looked at me so all my clothes were too big until one day I thought, you know what, no one is hitting me in the face right now, I'm going to buy this red dress from The Gap, I'm going to spend money I don't

have to do it, and so I did, and I went to a party on one of the Avenues feeling fancy and looking good and my friends were there and there was a balcony that wrapped around a corner and overlooked Central Park and people complimented me and my dress while I drank wine and I think there was coke; if there was coke

I did that too. One of our group was a man I'll call S who people thought was handsome in a James Dean way I guess if James Dean had lived past when James Dean had lived and had accrued enough alcohol in his liver that his skin had that kind of gray, puffy look lifetime drinkers might get although S was only around

30 at the time. We left the party to go to a second location and somehow it was only the two of us in the cab, me and S. Although I remember saying to a friend, *please ride with us*, I get how things happen when people are divvied up amongst cabs. Cabs are fancy and decisions have to be made and there was probably coke

and S always got just what S wanted. In the cab, S kept trying to move in on my mouth with his mouth and so I turned away, and he was okay with that, I think he didn't realize that was a *no*, only that he kept missing. *Look at you*, he said. *In that dress. Don't you know I have a girlfriend?* I did know and sometimes I felt sorry for her because, even if he didn't strike her in the face, S's skin was kind of gray for 30 and she seemed to tend to him the way I imagined 1950s women tended to their partners, helping them out of their shoes when drunk, emptying the ashtrays while they typed their tragic and male American wonderpieces. The next thing I

knew, S dove at me, his hand quick between my legs. I think it probably took a moment for me to realize what was going on, as often happens when a man is sexually assaulting me, so before I knew it his fingers were on my vulva and if he'd been less drunk and more coordinated his fingers would have been inside

me but luckily he was clumsy and not fully committed to the action and when I went to move his hand away he let me move his hand away. I made some light chatter in the cab to keep him occupied until we got to the second location and it was only when we arrived there that I allowed myself to feel anything at

all, though I wasn't sure exactly what it was I felt and I still don't know exactly what it was I felt. I think I waited to tell anyone what had happened but S continued to follow me around the second location, a friendlier one really, my friend's apartment, until my friend kicked him out for hounding me, and I was

relieved and grateful, and embarrassed about my curvy shape in my red dress. My friend walked a very drunk and nonsensical S to the subway where he passed out and rode the #2 line from the Bronx to Brooklyn back to the Bronx back to Brooklyn all night long and someone stole his wallet because how could they not

and then the story became *poor S got so drunk his wallet was stolen!* and *he's really a very disturbed genius, someone help him!* My friend said I should talk to him so I went to his place of work, which was behind a desk outside an art gallery and the chair sat sideways so I had to turn my body to face him. I said,

Do you remember what happened? and he said *no* and I said, *you grabbed my pussy in the cab* and he said, *Well come on! Don't act like you're not always flirty and seductive* and I tried to quietly sort out if I was always flirty and seductive. I ended up apologizing to S saying *I'm sorry you had to leave the*

party and that your wallet got stolen and he said *it's okay*, though he avoided me after that and told our friend that he couldn't respect me because I'm not a serious enough person.

NATIONAL PASTIME

Experience tells me
readers seem okay with poems about sexual violence

but more like sexy violence, which is to say

we want our victims with a cinched waist.
I'm getting a little bored with your ongoing fantasies.

Anything can be begged into art.

Most of my first wanted pregnancy I watched the Mets
on channel eleven while lying on my left side.

Much of my second wanted pregnancy wasn't during baseball season.
I watched a lot of kids' TV.

I cried every time Mister Rogers told me I had worth.

I appreciate how a game unfolds slowly
how little happens for innings and suddenly it's all happening.

I admire the relentless but practical hope
of every at bat.

A literary agent told me that rape is hot right now.

The other night I posted a purple sunset on Instagram
only to see everyone else's purple sunset across my phone

until suddenly what had astonished me seemed tacky.

Experience tells me
editors want to read my rape poems

until someone else sends rape poems
that are an extended metaphor

for this ancient god or that well known myth
and not a spirited description of what becomes of labia

when a man forces himself between.

What am I getting at? I have no solution, no vision
for the future. I can see you're turned on by my ruin.

(*Words that are heavy with nothing but trouble*)

What am I saying?

I'm saying: I'm not ruined, dirtbag.
I'm saying: we are no better, we who pretend to be better.

WHEN YOU LIE DOWN AND WHEN YOU RISE UP

From the time I was small I was told
we're unsafe, told *when they come back for us,*
when the Nazis come back for us

and it was impossibly rainless
the older I grew and the crisp
emptiness of the sidewalks shone back

into my smudged lenses
like an exclamation point and I was dazzled!
by America though I didn't know any other.

I didn't believe them
when they come back for us
while men tossed around anyone with an hourglass

and, the truth is, I was good on my knees,
I was so loved during if irrelevant after.
I was female. I was Jewish but I didn't believe

Nazis were coming back for us, our dead
left mid-century and now we're in an odd hour
of collapsing ease in the collective history so

I can't rid my tongue of all these syllables.
L'ahavah et Adonai Eloheikhem
ul'av'do b'khol l'vav'khem uv'khol naf'sh'khem.

I shudder at it sometimes, its trudging
cadence, but some all-night-longs it comforts me
like nothing more provocative can comfort me.

A man in a strip club once confessed to me
his fetish for Jewish women and for years now
I have wished I had asked him, under the angry

and merciless lights, the minacious pitch
of inexorable night, if the turn on
is more in the persecution, or in the resilience.

JULY 4, 2017

I went the long way to avoid a certain shopkeeper
who grunts at me

and instead I passed a street vendor
selling star-spangled towels and a tank top that reads

I HAVE NO TITS and I wish I was fearless
enough to ask who that shirt is meant for, and if,

at this point in time, we should even consider irony.
I've had tits for three decades

so I'm used to going the long way.
Fellow Americans,

I'm going to tell you something I've known
since childhood. Men who want to hurt you?

They want to hurt you
because it makes them feel good to hurt you.

Still, I'll admit, I woke up this morning so terribly sexy
at 43, one hand on my thigh the other

in my hair, that I almost didn't worry
a world past my own self.

I recognize my own fireworks.
Yankee Doodle, keep it up!

That whole song is about guns and women.
That whole song is about fragile masculinity.

Stop calling after me. The curve of my flesh
will not accommodate this hour in our history

and while many congrats on your glittering wit
and your stiff two-toned riding boot

on my throat, my fellow Americans,

I'm curious what combination of fear and admiration
makes a noise like father's gun, only a nation louder.

ZOLA BUDD IS NO MYTH

No myth I have no country.

No myth I am the fastest woman in the world.

No myth I run barefoot.

No myth I can't breathe deep enough—I need air—we all do—I do especially.

No myth I show up in Los Angeles like everyone shows up in Los Angeles: rosy.

No myth Mary Decker is the fastest woman in the world—Mary Decker is American— Oh, America! Oh, America. No myth.

No myth I am not made for pack running.

No myth my racist country persists. No myth yours does too.

No myth the boos by an American crowd in the land of dreams escalate when an eagle mascot lifts its wings to encourage the delirious crowd.

No myth a mourning dove lands on my windowsill trying to tell me no one knows me. If a pigeon appears it says no one remembers no myth.

No myth Mary Decker denies a doping charge.

No myth my neighbor stands behind her screen for hours, watching the street for signs of *other*. When she cracks the door, I don't know if it's to let air in or out.

No myth I am best known for collision.

No myth I forgot my groceries and a young woman chases after me. "You!" she says, "You!" And she catches me.

No myth sometimes there is money all over me. Money before country. Country before honor.

No myth I want what you want—air—I chase what you chase—air—I leave what you leave—dust.

Mostly I come from shtetl people except one great-great-someone who comes from banking money but who left to follow a saloon owner to lower Manhattan. Ah, love. Genetically, I'm programmed to put romance first. I'm a fainter.

Everyone who could speak Yiddish sentences to me is dead or doesn't remember me. I knew an Irish guy from the rust belt who learned Yiddish words listening between the misogyny of a Jewish shock jock.

Several intolerable Augusts ago I took a train to Division Street to find the saloon building. In its place was the Manhattan Bridge overpass. I overheated and had to cool down in the air of a dismal KFC.

So many in this city mourn its changes but I don't know what we do but keep going. That's another thing about genetics. I see in my children the entire transcript. I see in them a kind of hereafter.

RIPPED MOM

It became something I didn't recognize.
20+ hours of labor and my vulva swelled up

until I walked like a plastic cowboy from a vending machine
forever ready to ride.

I don't remember if doctors cut me or if I tore
and I didn't care and don't.

I've had no time for a hand mirror at my pussy.
I look for any instance of pleasure,

though everything I read said I was supposed to disarm.

We had a pretty good time together, when she wasn't
trying to kill me! but you can't stop me when

I am so turned on by my own damn self and so

exquisite down there.

A JEWISH CHRISTMAS IN PALM SPRINGS

If you ask me why all my poems
are the same I'll admit all my
impulses are sexual and all my
grudges are biblical. Skip my bio,
I'll just tell you: I took a woman
to the desert and she slapped
my red trap in a dander. I took
a man to the desert and he died
in front of me puffed up under
an obscene feast of stars muffled
by holiday strings of outsize bulbs
among the cacti. Sure, I'm duly
bowled by such grandeur but
I am asking you for patience
while I learn to say what I saw.

THE WHOLE WORLD IS THE BEST LAND I EVER LIVED

It's not that I don't remember
the pain of childbirth, it's that
maybe I needed it. Lately,

women are brave for saying
they hate being a mother
but I've gambled on all the pain

I will bring my babies
because I have loved nothing
more than mothering. When

finally we were alone, I saw
you study me from your plastic
bassinet and I knew you knew

my ambition. I was ashamed
by all the ways I will fail you and
then flown by your forgiveness.

When you were six, mornings
you'd look for one unbroken
leaf on our walk to school to hide it

so later we could find it again
walking home. That kind of faith.
Green then red then brown then

green again, proof of longing
and immutability. Often I was
impatient. Often we were hurried

or my mind was on an irrelevant
elsewhere. But you trusted me
to come back to you and be there.

Be. There. Each afternoon
we dug through the shallow leaf
graves, your fingers my fingers

but slowly distinct. I am sorry
I will have to be finite on your
wondrous and steadfast earth.

THE PATRON SAINT OF LOST THINGS

I married a man who taught me to laugh,
who acquainted me with saints

to throw suffering toward heaven. I'm sure
I'm getting this wrong but I prayed

to St. Anthony to find my passport
and he found it. I flew to Paris. I walked

to the Jewish quarter and ate strawberries
so sweet they slammed me against a wall

in ecstasy. I'm not exaggerating.
I was newlywedded in spring sunlight.

We are barely more than a century
out from Cossacks and here in America

there are rallies with Nazis chanting
"Jews will not replace us!" In Brooklyn,

a man opened a pogrom escape room.
I'm not kidding and I'm not into games.

St. Anthony, people complain
I'm too serious but history broke

my heart. Jewish bodies were weak bodies,
destroyed bodies. Jewish bodies were

resilient bodies, surviving bodies.
St. Anthony, if I make it back to that church

in Paris I will drop more coins into
the wooden box, light as many candles

as you need to floodlight the miracles,
St. Anthony, to illuminate what's missing.

TIME WILL CHANGE IT, I'M WELL AWARE

Maybe there are more orgasms in July
when the hot impossibility of existence

does the trick

but I'm writing to you from a bathtub

in January
in the middle of my life.

Used to be
spread under a faucet

arching up, weight on my elbows

hands rambling—
used to be that wouldn't leave me creaky the next day

but the secret is
I don't mind

and I prize sex bruises from porcelain.
I'm regal like that.

At noon when the sun intensifies

the glass, I stand before myself
pink, done, not done, never done,

half done, I guess.

TWELVE

When I was your age I went to a banquet.
When I was your age I went to a barroom

and bought cigarettes with quarters
lifted from the laundry money. Last night

I did all your laundry. I don't know why
I thought this love could be pure. It's enough

that it's infinite. I kiss your cheek when you sleep
and wonder if you feel it.

It's the same cheek I've kissed from the beginning.
You don't have to like me.

You just have to let me
keep your body yours. It's mine.

When I was your age I went to a banquet
and a man in a tux pinched my cheeks.

When I was your age I went to a barroom
and a man in a band shirt pinched my ass.

There is so much I don't know about you.
Last night I skipped a banquet

so I could stay home and do your laundry
and drink wine from my grandmother's glass.

When I was your age boys traded quarters
for a claw at my carcass on a pleather bench

while I missed the first few seconds of a song
I'd hoped to record on my backseat boombox.

When I was your age I enjoyed a hook.
You think I know nothing of metamorphosis

but when I was your age I invented a key change.
You don't have to know what I know.

REFUSENIK

I was promised a girl

held her glossy image, shatterable,

ice skating on a Soviet pond.

I'd never seen snow

but for the cut-out paper flakes

hung in school hallways.

I only knew rain

as intermittent confusion.

Los Angeles in the '80s.

We set fire to hairspray

for fun we wrote half-truths

in our padlocked journals,

we collected the phone numbers

of grown men we collected

the gratification of grown men

to trade for money,

we were adolescent!

There was never enough

money and there were never

any quiet moments on a pond

there was never any pond only

swimming pools into whose

water I was not invited.

I couldn't withstand the excess,

spent any money on bus fare

and lipstick and then,

then V showed up

on a plane from the Soviet Union

and was a boy, they told me

there was a mistake,

this beautiful 15-year-old boy

with his family

all arranged to stay with us.

+

When I was 10

there was a presidential primary

and I ate lunch at a table

by the stacks

and told the librarian

I would vote for Alan Cranston

mostly because he reminded me

of a doctor I saw

before we came to California,

an old white man,

gentle, gentile. My childhood

was littered

with white men, mostly Jewish,

the way the state park

was littered with chaparral

and cigarette butts,

so my childhood

was not spent wondering

if Jews are white,

there are white people

and there are Jews

but white Jews are white,

I would have said

if anyone had asked me

and anyway

my Jewish men

were rarely gentle.

His whole career,

Alan Cranston

advocated for the abolition

of nuclear weapons. The next year

Sting wrote a song

about mutual assured destruction

and so we all wondered

if Russians loved their children

too but at that point

I'd begun to wonder

about Americans

and gentleness

and who loved me

and I stopped

going to the library

and by the time I watched Sting

perform his song

on our black-and-white television

I'd started trading

tit feels for vodka

and stopped worrying

about Russians for a bit

and I don't think I thought

about Alan Cranston

again

until he died.

I wanted it all

to just stop but instead

I got tipsy

and learned capitalism,

learned

what a white female body

is worth

in liquid ounces.

+

When V and his family

found their own apartment

his mother didn't

want to unpack

the Judaica so we stuck it

under her bed.

We found some

of his mother's turquoise jewelry

and V wore it

at school, luminous

in the hair band '80s when

men could wear jewelry

and be pretty

but let's remind ourselves

that these pretty men

found my friends and me

up and down

Sunset and statutory

raped us in ways we felt

so good about until we didn't.

I skipped school

and V fingered me

on his mom's bed

like he wanted to comprehend

every part

and I was

not expecting to get off

anyway and later

we hid in the closet

when his mom came home

after looking for work

and we watched her

through the crack

of the door change

into something fancier,

watched her heft

her breasts

into her bra,

place her shoulder pads

in her blouse,

fix her makeup.

Awkward

and something

more than horny,

we watched

for womanhood.

+

In breaking news,

a Jewish candidate

is almost preferred to a shiksa

but the other white man

wins anyway

and of course.

In broken news, Jewish men

keep lecturing me about it

but give me points for sitting here.

If you were me

would you dramatically cover your ears?

I should be noticed

for some reason.

I listen to the table talk Russia,

talk white men, talk Jews

of history destroyed by blood

libel laws wherein it's said

we drink Christian blood.

I mean, I do that,

if you get what I'm saying.

Still,

I haven't turned a trick

for years. Let me be

clear, let me be more clear

than I was the last time

I wrote about this:

my Mexican friend K

was busted for walking

a street corner

she and I walked together

but only she

was flung in a jail cell

with less care than how

earlier we'd flung cans

over a fence to kill time

and then I was gently instructed

by a white officer to fly out

the side of the station

before being charged

with anything.

What was handed to me

but my whiteness

and my mouth, but that is why

I'm here, that is why

you see me at all, I seem

to need to remind everyone.

A man around this round table

in this library

sits wide-legged in his chair

and talks at me for 30 minutes

about Nazis

and oh wow, really?

Nazis, you say?

Never heard of it.

Never not until you told me.

+

"We Are the World"

won the Grammy for everything

in 1986 as we all knew it would

and it did

and Sting won nothing but did

perform "Russians" both patriotic

and subversive, which was a thing

in the '80s and anyway

almost all the nominees

in the top categories

were white men

and I didn't question it but

I'm sure

somebody somewhere did

in some archived page

in the coldest room

in the library written well

before I showed up.

My mistake has always been

in thinking I'm the center.

I thought I was pregnant,

which happened

about once a month

but this time

I really wondered

and I stood outside Thrifty's

while V bought me a pregnancy test

and I was 12

and not pregnant

and the woman at Thrifty's

thought V was a girl

and he was happy

but when I asked him

if he wanted me

to think he was a girl

he said *shut up*

and when I told him no

one wants to be treated like a girl

he said *screw you*

as if he'd been waiting months

to say that. I let him

fondle my breasts

in an empty stairwell

after I'd peed on the plastic test stick

and we watched the spill

of yellow downwards.

I'm not kidding when I tell you

"We Are the World" blasted

from at least two cars

circling the levels.

+

Blue eye shadow was big mid-decade

with me and also V's mom.

Time was,

you could put a dollar price tag

on a six dollar cosmetic

and the cashier wouldn't notice.

I tried all the colors.

Everything was an option.

Oh how I wanted things in the '80s!

Beaten-down denim.

Sleeves of rubber bracelets.

The used blue eye shadow

slipped into my pocket

while V's mom looked

through the paper for work.

I believed capitalism

could save my life. My peacock eyes

I thought could deliver assimilation.

+

In 1939, Hitler's publisher sued

Alan Cranston for publishing

an English translation

of *Mein Kampf* without erasing

the antisemitism.

You should know.

I grew up being told everyone hated us

but I saw no evidence of that

in Los Angeles,

only us hating ourselves.

We all believed the stereotypes.

V and I sat

outside a Purim carnival

smoking thin cigarettes

riffing on the danger

we'd put ourselves in.

I wanted everyone to stop

howling about how

much I'd survived

and I still want this.

I let V start to stub out

the dig-end on my forearm.

I don't know who I am,

he said.

V threw a bean bag at a target

and accepted a goldfish.

I'm telling you this

because V named the fish Hitler,

though he told his mother

he'd named it Spot.

Even he'd become that comfortable.

+

In daily news,

I am full of vengeance

because I was born

with the Old Testament

in my veins. The curator

for Jewish texts couldn't look me

dead on because maybe

I talked about my pussy

too many times

in my presentation

at the flagship library

where I am being paid

to write about Jews.

I said why don't we stop

pretending modern Judaism

gives a nod to women

when on the wall of the last shul

I stepped into

that called itself feminist

a sign carved into the stone read

"Have We Not All One Father?"

and unless you take a chisel to it

I am done.

In 1988, I told V I was nothing

if not Jewish

and I knew I meant it

and I know I mean it now.

+

V began to scorn me,

my form, my city. A wall

came down

and Americans felt so superior,

dangerous. Caustic

rays shone and shone

onto Fairfax Avenue

where I stood in my dayglo

bikini top

asking for money.

I was happy in my old life, V said.

We sat outside

CBS studios and smoked a joint

I'd seduced a stranger

into handing over

and V and I walked

to the shul

on Olympic for a basement

reception for Soviet Jews

where the women wore boots

studded in rhinestones

that outshone what had once

been fancy place settings

and everyone

was really very proud

of themselves

and Jews and America

and I felt stoned

and cocky and breathlessly

I marveled,

We are living through history!

and V said,

I never want to see you again.

+

Because,

in the end,

the flora of Los Angeles

will make you gasp

every few steps

because it's outlandish

and sharp

and you always forget

how beautiful

the way you forget

the intensity of pain

because it's all unbearable,

like the sun

of Southern California

which burned and still burns

our white skin quick

as white Jews are white

but with an asterisk because Nazis

march against us

and Russians plot a takeover

while politicians look away.

Alan Cranston was publicly

reprimanded

in 1991 for something

to do with money.

Have I touched enough

on money here?

It's all that any of this was ever about,

though

it's always about power

my colleagues will correct me,

as ever,

to sum up.

+

When I ran into V

the last time on a street corner

in 1990, surrounded

by the glorious excess

we scarred ourselves

trying to burn down

we kind of laughed

about all of it and he said

just two ladies of the night!

because V was always proud

to use an idiom.

The air smelled of eucalyptus

and spice

from a Mexican market

with its doors thrown open

into the pleasure of the plashing air

in whatever season that was

and V touched my arm gently

and told me about how at night

back home in winter

it was so gravely hushed

that your every

insufficient exhalation

could actually matter

the world around you.

TIKKUN OLAM

46 and out on a Friday night
in the stiletto boots I waited months to buy

because I'm cheap but
that's a dangerous cliché to use

given what's been said of Jews and
Are Jews people?

cable news asked me one morning
and don't think I haven't ripped out

my own heart to stop it from beating
back a confused reply.

One day I woke up and I couldn't digest.
Last summer it hurt to close my fist.

The diner waiter keeps asking me
if I have enough. Is it enough? What is enough?

I love you.
I'm over-dressed even for a soliloquy

even for a Valentine's Day
even on Shabbat

especially for the tables in this diner—
that's laminate you're leaning on,

Lynn, not marble!—
where I first blurted the wish

that started all of this. The night is new.
The night shows me a sky

I do not deserve (both wanton
and elegant, me in my boots, the sky)

and which I'd never seen before,
not really, not before you held my hand

across the laminate,
even though it has been up there

biding its time my entire life.
You touch my leg under the table.

You order pie. I'm here to talk about humanity
and all I can think about is how you look

at me. The Mishnah tells us together
we must repair the world

and still I have little faith in a god
who gives us this, yes, perfect

moon slinking through skyscrapers
into the diner, as if that's enough.

THIS FALL

I wear a moth-eaten sweater dress
and refuse to speak in metaphor.
One of these days I will sew up the holes.
One of these days

I will learn how to sew
so I can sew up the holes.
I do things with my body
I am ashamed to tell you about

but not ashamed to have done.
I go into and out of
the city on the subway.
I am already in the city but

I go into the center.
People like to ask me for directions
so we can get lost together.
I await word

from a love in the hospital
but word doesn't come.
I am trolled on Twitter
for complaining about men.

Is it too early in the century to write
trolled on Twitter into a poem
because I'm pretty sure *trolled on Twitter*
will be in my obituary

and in that of our century.
I'm wearing it well, moth-eaten.
They think I think
I'm too good for men, which

I have always been. Still,
I find myself opening my heart.
I would like to be rescued
from these feelings

while I resist revealing
what it feels like in a body
awaiting word and waiting
for my husband

to get home from the city.
My challenge is to stop bracing
for the worst. We are lost.
Every love like all of us will die.

I will never get word.
I will wait and wait
for my husband to arrive
with the vindictive wind

into the fourth floor of what is also
the city. I'm bleeding
more than I ever have,
each bleed worse than the last,

my immoderate body
at the crest of things. I'm bleeding
in abundance onto my dress
and onto the couch.

When I was in school I wrote
a poem called "Blood Stains."
My teacher wrote *not quite*
across the top

but blood does stain, quite.
On Twitter a man calls me ugly.
On Twitter another man
calls me a bitch.

I've never been either
but I could stand to be both.
I wait obsessively for word.
I am invincible and

I am so sorry, Twitter.
I hear news—
I hear news!—
from the hospital: *I'm ok.*

I feel my body relax
inside the waning
worst-case-scenario reel.
This is the century *overwhelm*

became a noun, isn't it?
If my heart has to be open let it
at least sometimes receive relief.
I peel off my dress at the kitchen sink.

My husband walks in
and my body unspools further.
If I ask him, he will know how
to stitch the hole in my dress.

I told you I'm not speaking in metaphor.
I warned you we are all going to die.

LISTEN,

recently a mess of writers said it's the mark of an amateur to use this imperative to start a line in a poem but they weren't poets and I would like to be an amateur all my life. I mean, what happens when we get good at this? When we get too good? When we get so proficiently *fine* that our words go down easy? I do not want easy pain or easy beauty. It takes very little for me to lean back on the grass in sunshine because my head has long tried to split from my body, but I'm here on a wooden stool in the part of February almost past love. Brick walls, pleasant chatter, so much to get done and how lucky I am that I get to try. Everything is pretend. Everything is dead serious. Listen, when I write poems again, I want them to be about joy.

Notes

The title of "The Night of the Murdered Poets" refers to the night of August 12, 1952, during which thirteen Soviet Jewish intellectuals were executed in a prison basement in Moscow on charges of treason and espionage. The Sh'ma is regarded by many Jews as the most important prayer, as it serves as a reminder that there is only one God.

The weddings referred to in "The Only Jew at the Mock Jewish Wedding" are often held in parts of Europe by non-Jews, where there is nostalgia for the now nearly-extinct Jewish communities there. The word "treyf" is the Yiddish word for non-Kosher food. "Shtetl" is the Yiddish word for any of the small towns with large Jewish populations which existed in Central and Eastern Europe before the Holocaust. This poem is for Anita and Michael Melnick.

"When Bad Things Happen to Good People" takes its title from the title of the 1981 book by Harold Kushner, a Conservative rabbi.

"Satan in Goray" takes its title from the novel of the same name by Isaac Bashevis Singer.

"We'd Like to Know a Little Bit About You for Our Files" takes its title from a line in the Simon & Garfunkel song "Mrs. Robinson." "Shiksa" is the Yiddish word for a non-Jewish girl or woman. "Shegetz" is the Yiddish word for a non-Jewish boy or man.

The events in "Glasnost Bowl" describe a planned attempt to stage an American college football game (between the University of Southern California and the University of Illinois) in the Soviet Union at the beginning of the 1989 season.

It was named after the term "glasnost" (a term introduced by then Soviet leader Mikhail Gorbachev in 1985) and means "openness." Due to complications with infrastructure, the game was ultimately moved to the USC ball field in Los Angeles. The word "goyim" is the Yiddish word for non-Jewish people.

"Cannibal Island" takes its title from the documentary of the same title directed by Cédric Condon regarding an incident in 1933 where Stalin ordered thousands of unwanted citizens of the Soviet Union to be moved against their will to a small, isolated island in Western Siberia.

"Too Jewish / *shtetl kitsch*" borrows some lines from the musical *Fiddler on the Roof* by Joseph Stein, and takes the latter half of its title from Philip Roth, who dismissed the play as such. This poem is for Barbara White.

"Why, Because the Dazzling Sun" takes its title from the Emily Brontë poem "Ah! Why, Because the Dazzling Sun."

The italicized line in "National Pastime" come from the 1910 poem, "Baseball's Sad Lexicon" by Franklin Pierce Adams.

The Hebrew lines in "When You Lie Down and When You Rise Up" translate to "to love the Lord your God and to serve him with all your heart and all your soul" which is from the Sh'ma prayer, from which the title of the poem also comes.

The last line of "July 4, 2017" comes from a line in the American folk song "Yankee Doodle."

"Zola Budd Is No Myth" takes its title from something BBC's commentator, David Coleman, exclaimed about the South African runner after an Olympicqualifying race in 1984: "The message will now be flashed around the world. Zola Budd is no myth."

The italicized lines in "Ripped Mom" come from something John Wayne said in 1954, in an interview with Hedda Hopper regarding his marriage to Esperanza Baur.

The poem "The Whole World Is the Best Land I Ever Lived" takes its title from a sentence my daughter spoke to me. This poem is for Stella Donnelly.

"Time Will Change It, I'm Well Aware" takes its title from a sentence in Emily Brontë's *Wuthering Heights*: "My love for Linton is like the foliage in the woods: time will change it, I'm well aware, as winter changes the trees."

"Twelve" is for Ada Donnelly.

The word "shul," in the poem "Refusenik," is the Yiddish word for synagogue. The holiday Purim commemorates a woman named Esther who saved the Jewish people from Haman, an ancient Persian Empire official who was hoping to kill all the Jews.

"Tikkun Olam" takes its title from the Jewish concept of acts of kindness performed to repair the world. The "Mishnah" is a collection of Jewish oral traditions and laws.

Acknowledgments

Grateful acknowledgment to the editors of the venues in which many of these poems previously appeared: *Academy of American Poets's Poem-a-Day, The Adroit Journal, American Poetry Review, The Awl, BOAAT, Boston Review, Brink, Brooklyn Magazine, E3, ESPN, Glass Poetry, LIT, Los Angeles Review of Books, Lyra, The Rumpus, Poetry, Poetry Daily, A Public Space, Unterberg Poetry Center.*

"Inauguration Poem" ("Do you know what it's like . . .") was included in the anthology *Poems for Political Disaster* (Boston Review) & as part of The Poetry Project's Poetry Canon project.

"National Pastime" was included in the anthology *Who Will Speak for America?* (Temple University Press).

"Migration" was included in the anthology *A New Colossus* (Unterberg Poetry Center).

This book would not be possible without the time, space, cohort, and resources afforded me by the New York Public Library's Cullman Center for Scholars and Writers. Thanks particularly to Lauren Goldenberg, who reminded me early on that I deserved to be there as much as everyone else, and to fellow Fellow Melinda Moustakis, who checked in with me in so many ways.

This book benefitted from the time afforded by a generous grant from the Hadassah-Brandeis Institute. I am hugely grateful for the support and faith in my work.

For the steadfast support and wisdom of KMA Sullivan: endless gratitude. Also to the entire YesYes Books team, especially cover wizard Alban Fischer.

I owe so much of my durability to the love, faith, and advice of my friends. Thank you Brett Fletcher Lauer, for reading everything I write. Thank you Marina Blitshteyn, for the crucial conversations. And to Barbara White, for understanding.

Thank you to the impossibly sharp Kate Colby, who read every word of every version of this book, and cut me no slack. Thank you to the impossibly honest Jess Workman, who knows every part of my life, and cuts me no slack.

To V and K, hopefully safe, wherever you are now.

To the late Phil Bosakowski, ever.

To Timothy Donnelly, *everything and always*, always, and to Ada Donnelly, and to Stella Donnelly. My heart beats your names.

PHOTO BY ADA DONNELLY

LYNN MELNICK is the author of the poetry collections *Refusenik* (2022), *Landscape with Sex and Violence* (2017), and *If I Should Say I Have Hope* (2012), all with YesYes Books, and the co-editor of *Please Excuse This Poem: 100 Poets for the Next Generation* (Viking, 2015). Her memoir, *I've Had to Think Up a Way to Survive: On Trauma, Persistence, and Dolly Parton* is forthcoming from the University of Texas Press in 2022.

ALSO FROM YESYES BOOKS

FICTION
Girls Like Me by Nina Packebush

FULL-LENGTH COLLECTIONS
Ugly Music by Diannely Antigua
Gutter by Lauren Brazeal
What Runs Over by Kayleb Rae Candrilli
This, Sisyphus by Brandon Courtney
Salt Body Shimmer by Aricka Foreman
Forever War by Kate Gaskin
Ceremony of Sand by Rodney Gomez
Undoll by Tanya Grae
Loudest When Startled by Lukas Ray Hall
Everything Breaking / For Good by Matt Hart
Sons of Achilles by Nabila Lovelace
Landscape with Sex and Violence by Lynn Melnick
GOOD MORNING AMERICA I AM HUNGRY AND ON FIRE
    by jamie mortara
Stay by Tanya Olson
a falling knife has no handle by Emily O'Neill
To Love An Island by Ana Portnoy Brimmer
One God at a Time by Meghan Privitello
I'm So Fine: A List of Famous Men & What I Had On by Khadijah Queen
If the Future Is a Fetish by Sarah Sgro
Gilt by Raena Shirali
Say It Hurts by Lisa Summe

Boat Burned by Kelly Grace Thomas

Helen Or My Hunger by Gale Marie Thompson

RECENT CHAPBOOK COLLECTIONS

Vinyl 45s

   Inside My Electric City by Caylin Capra-Thomas

   Exit Pastoral by Aidan Forster

   Of Darkness and Tumbling by Mónica Gomery

   The Porch (As Sanctuary) by Jae Nichelle

   Juned by Jenn Marie Nunes

   Unmonstrous by John Allen Taylor

   Preparing the Body by Norma Liliana Valdez

   Giantess by Emily Vizzo

Blue Note Editions

   Beastgirl & Other Origin Myths by Elizabeth Acevedo

   Kissing Caskets by Mahogany L. Browne

   One Above One Below: Positions & Lamentations by Gala Mukomolova

Companion Series

   Inadequate Grave by Brandon Courtney

   The Rest of the Body by Jay Deshpande